ON THE RECORD

By the same author:

Peripheral Vision (2018)
Sleeping Dogs (2020)

ON THE RECORD

MARTIN DOLAN

RECENT
WORK
PRESS

On the Record
Recent Work Press
Canberra, Australia

Copyright ©Martin Dolan 2023

ISBN: 9780645651256 (paperback)

A catalogue record for this
book is available from the
National Library of Australia

Cover image: Martin Dolan
Cover design: Recent Work Press
Set by Recent Work Press

recentworkpress.com

ss

To the ancestors, with thanks for the stories.

Contents

On the record	1
William S	3
William Y	4
Michael	5
Hector Macdonald	6
Isabella	7
Katie	8
Archie	9
Christina	10
Nancy	11
George	13
Bridget	15
Alan	16
Rodger	18
Harvey Littlejohn	20
William D	21
James	23
Robert	24
Eleanor	25
Annie	27
Bessie	28
Christian	29
John	30
Philip	31

On the record

Both entries are firm, showing no doubt:
'drowned in canal, suicide';
'overdose of laudanum'.
Then ages: sixty-five and sixty.

Thus two ancestors were disposed of
by the same doctor, ten years
and half a city apart;
in an asylum, a third lived on.

Other papers and a closer eye
sketch answers not sought out then:
husbands dead, sons at the war
long years of dirt and grinding work

and, locked away, the single mother
whose heart would give out at last
long after her mind had left;
her daughter elsewhere, respectable.

William S

Helensburgh, 18 June 1869. Congestion; haemorrhage of bowels

You can be so tired that it hurts
blunt and solid behind your eyes
pulse beating like thump of mallet
on chisel as you shape rough stone.
You can be so tired you sleep
when you should have walked away from
children's squabbles, wife's reproaches
walked in the cold night for a while
breath in clouds before you, beard wet.
I shaped my father's gravestone, carved
his name, the dates. It was good work.
There's a piece of stone in the yard
will do for mine. Who will carve it?
Young Willie's gone for a soldier,
Archie to the excise. And Jock
the prentice does not have the gift
of care after a long day's work.
I'd do it with these old, stiff hands
if I could get out of this bed.
I still have the skill, the tools
but it is dark. I am so tired.

William Y

Knockando, 22 Mar 1899. Influenza; cerebral apoplexy

The spring is coming in, the smell of gorse
is everywhere. Smells like coconuts,
my grandson says, back from the army
and India, but that means nothing
to me. Gorse smells of gorse, spring flowers
yellow among the prickles. Winter
we hack it back from our drystone dikes,
rake it in piles ready for burning,
but it spreads wild on the braes, choking
grass and heather. In our fields, barley
is standing, is running up the slope with the wind.
Too dark to see it now, where we ploughed
and harrowed, the horses working hard,
urged on by our voices. Too dark to see,
the sun behind the ridge long ago,
yellow lights now down in the valley,
dotted along the river, marking
the narrow streets, the station.
No lights on the opposite hillside,
just darkness stretching up to the sky,
to half-seen clouds, a handful of stars.
I do not think I will see barley
set its ears, or scythes mowing, harvest.
This fever will not give. A cold wind

Michael

Edinburgh, 4 January 1904. Pulmonary phthisis

It is winter dark. The room is cold.
Bridget is not here. I do not know
why she has left me. The fire burns low
and badly. The air smells of sulphur
as though Rodger was lighting matches
for play or as though I was at work
carrying rubber boots from their moulds
to the ovens to harden. Sulphur
in the air, our clothes, everywhere
and us coughing as we work, coughing
as we shuffle in line to our shift,
coughing as we pass the gates, head home
in the dark, back to our little rooms.
The coal man has cheated us. The fire
should warm the room and it should not stink.
It is dark. I cannot see the time,
or see Bridget to ask is it time
to get up and dress so I can go to work.
It is so difficult to get dressed,
walk to the factory in the cold.
Always coughing, gobs of phlegm
and now blood, the handkerchief useless.
The coughing was too much for Bridget,
she couldn't sleep, she's in the next room,
I remember now, she needs her sleep.
Make it stop, the coughing. It's so hard
to draw a breath or to fall asleep.
I'll lie here and wait. Maybe she'll come

Hector Macdonald

Attending physician

Twenty years and still the same knocking
in the wee hours, the same unkempt man,
shuffling and downcast, wanting me to come
with him to the same dark tenement
or another just like it. Someone
is dying or has already died
out of reach of my best endeavours
but I put on my coat, take my bag
and follow him through the winter dawn,
along wet streets, boots slipping on the dung
spattered across cobbles, dodging carts
and barrows up to the weathered door,
up two slippery flights of worn stairs
into the usual sitting room
and the usual cramped, close bedroom.
Before I examine him I know
there is nothing I can do, nothing
I could have done for six months or more
but there are motions I must go through,
the ritual of checking for life,
pronouncing it extinct and noting
the blood and sputum on the pillow.
Consumption, as once we called it,
coughs, blood, pale fading, death. I will go home,
certify pulmonary phthisis
in approved form. I did not know him.
He was already cold to my touch.

Isabella

Aberlour, 27 February 1904. Influenza; bronchial asthma

Night again. It has been dark so long:
only the moonlight through the curtain gap
and the lamp turned low. A winter night.
Frosty, he said, the skies clear. But here
with coal fire, blankets and my fever
it is so hot I can hardly breathe
as if I had been running too long.
No longer. I lie here in a sweat,
listening to my rough breath, my cough,
the coals crackling a little, horses
clopping outside, clink and creak of tack.
Maybe David made it, made their tack
and I sold it in our shop, wrote down
how much they paid. Now puff, screech and puff
as the train stops, hiss of steam, voices,
barrels rumbling along, hoops grinding,
thumped aboard, doors grate and are slammed shut
the steam puffing once twice and again
the train running by the riverside
to Daluaine, Carron and Knockando
my breath going with it, in and out,
smell of coal smoke the train noise gone.
I want to run again and I can't
blankets so heavy, not enough breath.

Katie

Edinburgh, 4 September 1905. Apparent overdose of laudanum

My throat so sore my sides my chest my head aches
the coughing will not stop everything is grey
and sore Willie brings my medicine again
the bottle brown small the cork easily out
drops red-brown bitter as always and I cough
and cough and drink the bitter liquid and cough
and Willie brings me tea sweetened with sugar
the cough goes away the afternoon is bright
lovely and wrapped close in familiar bedclothes
and Willie still there creases between his eyebrows
always that look when he brings me my medicine
so silly the cough is gone the warm feeling
sits in my stomach always so wonderful
to feel well to feel happy all pains all gloom
gone out where there is sunlight and leaves sleepy
my head the room spinning Willie in his chair
pins and needles in my feet my hands all numb
I cannot feel my hands in the corner shadows
gather together they are looking at me
they are laughing it is hard to breathe so hard

Archie

Helensburgh, 30 November 1905. Hemiplegia (left)

The devil's hand, they said. Sinister,
that's what the Latin master said.
In the playground I was cack-handed,
cack-footed when kicking at the ball.
What a kick, though: weight over ball,
the unexpected drive, the goalie sprawled.
In class the teachers won: pain flashing
across the knuckles of my left hand,
harsh cane slashing down on the fingertips
forbidden a pencil. Teachers won:
you can see it in the letter there
scrawled, half-legible, still unfinished,
work of my weaker, clumsier hand.
The heart's hand, I said when I met you,
held it out to meet yours. The heart's hand
because on the heart's side, closest to you.
Now the dead hand, limp, unmoveable
as my left leg, left side of my face.
I lie here, betrayed by my strong side,
good hand. The doctor waits on my heart.

Christina

Aberlour, 31 October 1912. Old age

Stop fussing around me. Stop stroking
my hand, flapping that cloth in my face.
All I want is to be left alone,
to sleep on this soft bed. Much softer
than the damp straw pallet in our croft
winter nights when the peats burned to ash
and the wind found chinks in our stone walls
and pushed at the thatch. Leave me alone
so I can find the summer again,
wind smoothing the barley like cat's fur,
sheep bleating behind the drystone walls
that Da and Angus Mor stacked with care.
Grass on the sunny side of the wall
and me looking up at how the clouds
wiped across the blue sky like soft rags
and beside me. And beside me. What
was his name and where is he gone to?
Stop buzzing about me like the flies
about the dead ewe, its neck broken
there in the bottom of the corrie,
its eyes taken by crows. Let me sleep
so I can run through spring, steal apples
from autumn, nurse my baby and feel
how strongly he sucks. He was so hot
with fever and then. What was his name?
The sound that the brush makes as it scrubs,
the stone floors cold except by the fire,
the kettle boiling. Stop your fussing
and let me remember your name. Stop

Nancy

Edinburgh, 3 December 1912. Brain haemorrhage

The candle gutters the wax wasting down
Dear Mother how the nib catches the page
this paper that I took from the bureau
that is the name they said I have the key
I hope you are well but she is not
they have taken her to that awful place
outside the town *as I am.* my bed
will soon be warm when I am finished here
The work is easy the same as home.
but they watch me with their narrow eyes
and their son so angry and so strong
I eat well and they pay me every month
the dance hall the lights so warm a drink
and then another the little band
plays so fast and loud *I can go out*
each Saturday. They ask me to dance
one another and a third until
that one keeps on dancing with me
and we stop and he buys me a drink
The church is nearby and I go there
each Sunday. it is cold they are stern
and stare as though I do not belong
among their fine clothes and buttoned coats
I have made good friends that is enough
she does not need to know what I feel
warm in my bed at night *and I am*
happy here. the candle will not last
much longer. *My love to you all. Your*

affectionate daughter so little to say
so much I will not say my cheeks hot
walking through the cold house to my bed.

George

Festubert, 16 May 1916. Killed in action

These mornings of clutching cold,
frost sparkling as it catches
thin sunlight, I can see steam
rise above the latrines there:
men in field grey piss, unseen.
This steel loophole has distilled
pure cold from the night and gnaws
gloved fingers as they scrabble
numbly towards their purpose.
They are so distant, those hands,
disconnected, driven by
the spring of their own clockwork.
One takes the sack-wrapped barrel
of the rifle, the other
works the bolt, smoothly, then drops
to wait, loose on the trigger.
The cross-hairs shift, curious,
seeking oddness in the white.
Shadows move, clockwork fingers
squeeze, a head explodes, red spray.
That was not my eye searching
not me in those hands. The job
is over, done, done again.

Bridget

Edinburgh, 22 September 1916. Drowning (suicide)

Alan

Witness

The sunlight is everywhere now
it glitters slick from the wet cobbles
makes oily rainbows on the canal.

Sun everywhere until the bridge
hulks over the water, drops shadow
on the half-warmth of early morning

and I hunch down into my collar
whiskers scratching, wind cold on my cheeks
breath sour with the smell of last night's beer

feet slow, shuffling to the day's drudge
past a moored barge, its cables creaking,
the flat water slopping against its boards

and there under the bridge near the bank
a bundle of cloth floats and jostles
discarded, unowned, now maybe mine

and of some worth to the rag merchant
if only the clocks were not chiming
the factory less hard on lateness.

I kneel anyway, knees cold on stone
reaching down hands cold wet to the wrists
turning a wet mass over looking

not seeing then seeing not rags face
eyes there is a body in my hands
looking not looking at me the sky

Rodger

Informant of death

All night the twins were bawling, screaming
and Jeanie did nothing to stop them
my head splitting, throat like sandpaper
and always the cough till ribs are sore
black phlegm and spitting who'd be a sweep
and bacon greasy eggs black pudding
staggering out into morning sun
pawing the grit of sleep from my eyes
up to Morningside with the brushes
clattered on my shoulders and always
coal smoke heavy in the morning air
feet shuffle autumn leaves red yellow
the servants' entrance the maid sneering
at clothes sooted and sweated with work
the work finished for a few small coins
the next house chimneys cough and spitting
phlegm into gutters where the leaves slide
underfoot as the rain comes and goes
and at last finished stop for a drink
at the Canny Man before Jeanie
and the twins still crying the loud knock
the constable looming at the door
holding my elbow through the gaslight
the Infirmary in the cold dark
sharp smells carbolic formaldehyde
my hobnails clattering on wooden floors
the doorway the white tiles white light
the shape under the white sheet drawn back

and it's her with lined face grey hair eyes closed
it's her I should not have wished her dead

Harvey Littlejohn

Examining physician

This one was simple. So many cases
that it becomes boring and everyday, body
after body on the cold slab, the rinsing
but no, first examine the mouth and the nose
for froth. It is there, fine and white. The simplest
indicator of drowning. The hands are clenched
but around nothing. No evidence from that.
The palms and fingers are hard and rough, the nails
ragged, cracked. Doubtless my father would have made
some deduction as to employment but I
am tired of cleverness. And so she is washed.
I take the scalpel in search of evidence.
There in the throat more froth. What more must I do?
Her son said that she had changed these last few years.
Incision down the chest. Shears to open ribs
so the lungs are freed. They are large, full of water
and when dissected also show deposits
and occlusions. No need for speculation.
This is a drowning in the dark before dawn
near home. And a mind that may have been disturbed.
This one was simple. Drowning. I write it down.
Next to that: suicide. In parentheses.

William D

Edinburgh, 22 October 1918. Heart disease

I could make the hammer fall just so
to bend tinplate around the anvil.
Tack tack. So many years tapped away.
So many hammers: chasing, creasing,
planishing, setting down. And mallets
wooden, clumsy—or bone for fine work.
I'll think on them rather than the pain
that grips my hammer arm and makes it
useless as the little bits of tin
fallen away from the snipper's blades.
Hammers and stakes and the shears that sliced
thin sheets of metal. Sharp shears and sharp
edges of cut tin. Always file them,
he said when I was a prentice lad,
always wear gloves. Still I sliced my hand
there was blood everywhere but no pain,
not at first. On cold mornings the scar
still aches, the finger I hammered wrong
aches and is as useless as this arm.
I'll think on the fire pot and solder,
hot iron, smell of ammonia
and tin overlapped on tin, made whole.
I made so many buckets and pans,
basins, pails, and pots. The new ones sold,
the old came back with their dents and holes
that I could mostly mend, even though
there was so little money in the work.
I could mostly fix that but I don't know how

to brace this dangled arm, patch up this chest
to protect this heart that falters, stops.

James

Edinburgh, 5 November 1919. Pulmonary tuberculosis

I can't remember when I wasn't coughing,
when I didn't have to work to catch a breath.
Maybe when it was just horse and cart and me
clopping over the wet cobbles, iron wheels
grinding, slipping on the muck of morning streets.
I didn't cough then. I whistled and I sang,
my breath puffing out into the nippy air.
When I courted Lizzie, climbing steep alleys
to the back door of the dancehall. No coughing
as we stepped and turned to music. Only heat
of movement, dizziness of dance and drink,
a sore head on the driver's seat next morning.
When we were married and when the children came
and the horse and cart were gone and the lorry
roared and the gears ground and everything was fast
I was coughing then, hawking up phlegm, spitting
my lungs into the morning and the wee ones
were lying in fever, sweating and dying.
I was coughing then. And war came and I signed
my X and drove the lorries for them, the mud
flying behind us, shells exploding in front
gas shells and where was my mask, the wheels slipping
the lorry bogged. Yes, we were all coughing then.
And now in this place where I have never been
this hospital with its clean walls, clean nurses
and me coughing not phlegm but blood on clean sheets
my lungs tearing and burning just make it stop

Robert

Invercargill, 20 October 1920. No cause given

Regret? That's an odd word to think on.
We have been happy here, you and I.
I see you're smiling. It must be true.
Seasickness. Why do I think of that?
Days of pitching, rolling, the ship's bow
hissing through the waves, crashing into troughs
and me at the rails, retching. It stopped
in the end. I remember clear skies
and sun as we ran before the wind.
Ran to the other side of the world
that looked like home under the grey rain,
or so we said. A half-truth at best.
Labour that cracked my hands, clearing trees
and grubbing stumps. My back still feels it,
still feels the work of crutching, shearing,
building yards, building this very house.
There's no regret in that. There's sadness
that we had no bairns, no one to leave
this place to when we're gone. I wonder,
some nights, what happened to ma and da,
whether they got the money I sent,
the communion cup, too, all silver.
Do they use it at kirk on Sundays.
So much left behind and that lassie,
what was her name? Bessie. Yes, that's it.
And the bairn she said was mine. Annie.
Not mine. I told them at kirk sessions.
I remember how they looked at me.
Not mine. Tell me we've been happy here.

Eleanor

Helensburgh, 27 April 1921. Arterial sclerosis; cholecystitis

It's as though pain brings them out
silent on the edge of sight,
crying where I can't see them,
can't tell what comes from hunger
what from pain they will never
learn any words to express.
They were born out of my pain
then left, cold, white, with the names
we had given them, the names
they would never grow into—
Maggie and Davie, Charlie—
the names that we took and gave
to others to grow into.
Why do they come, small and dead
and crying, when the others—
still warm, still lively—do not.
I don't want to be alone
on this spring night, the coal fire
whispering into grey ash,
alone with only the cries
of dead babies and the waves
of pain that roll across me
like I was birthing again
though I know I am too old
that Archie is dead who lay
with me in this bed and made
love, made babies, so many babies.
It hurts in my side, my chest.

The dead babies are gone, leaving
their pain behind. If I call
who will come to comfort me?

Annie

Inveravon, 5 November 1926. Bronchitis; cardiac degeneration

Her cheeks were hot, red in the dying firelight.
She looked straight at me, hardly blinking, her pupils
wide, breathing a little faster as she told
my story again. I can still feel its shape,
its rhythm like her breathing, the certainty
that this was truth: the fiddles and foot-tapping
on the wood floors of a church hall, the laughter
that perhaps came from quick drams taken outside
perhaps from the warmth of bodies and dancing
that kept on to the end of summer twilight
and the hay in the mown field and the fumbling
the smell of damp earth and the smell of him
the pleasure pain and the whispered promises
walking home alone saying his name over
and over like a spell no like a prayer
and her growing belly and him gone away
with promise to come back that was never kept
how she gave me his name though his family
would not own me how I was born out of love.
Never forget this. Her eyes staring at me.

Bessie

Banff, 28 January 1927. Cardio arterio sclerosis

My feet are cold. The wind outside, coming in.
It was a long road to school. My feet got wet.
I played with Peggy in the farmyard. Puddles.
We splashed in puddles after the rain had stopped.
Ma was so angry. This bed is wrong. Too hard
and scratchy. The blankets stink. The wind comes through
the window sash. The wind grabbed us as we walked,
tore Peggy's bonnet off. Robbie tore my clothes.
I had to mend them in the byre. The lamplight.
Why is the door rattling? The wind will not stop.
My teeth are chattering. My sisters chattered
and smiled behind their hands. No smiles from my Ma.
Pa hit me. Book learning had taught me nothing.
She was such a pretty thing, little Annie.
Not my girl. My wee sister. I went to work
in the farmhouse. My sister. Ma cared for her.
Where is she? She should be here to make me warm.
I want to go home. This is not home. It is wrong.
It is cold. It is so cold and no-one comes.

Christian

Informant of death

They don't pay me enough and the food is bad,
bad as what we give the inmates: a thin porridge,
too much salt, that we spoon into toothless mouths,
or slimy broths made from old vegetables.
Not enough to scrape shit from mattress ticking
though I do it every day as they curl, frightened,
empty, on the cold edge of their metal beds.
Always cold and the damp everywhere, the wind
snivelling at the window. She is crying
there on the edge of her bed. She wants to know
why she is here and if I am her sister
and when are we going home. She is as old
as my grandmother and my sister is dead.
I tell her to hush, it's not time yet to go.
I pull the blanket over her and close the door.

John

Inverary, 4 December 1942. Fracture to base of skull, hastened by exposure and cold

Philip

Witness at inquiry

Of course we were drinking. That's what pubs are for
after a winter's day learning how to kill
so that we wouldn't have in think about it
when the time came. A grey day. Dreich. There was snow
up in the mountains and the cold searched us out.
So cold the sergeant-major stopped his shouting
and whispered to us how to slide the knife in,
how to swing the cosh and just where it should hit.
The cosh was my weapon. Smash in their temple
or the back of their skull. I didn't like knives
the way John did. You get too close to a man
when you use a blade, so close you can feel them,
breath hot on your cheek. Yes, John preferred the knife.
And so we were all drinking, always drinking
the whisky warming our guts, heating our thoughts
and John got too close to one of us. I won't
say who it was. He punched John and John walked out
into the cold. We staggered back to barracks.
We didn't miss him until morning parade.
We went searching. I found him first, by the loch.
Face down. Dead. Cold as the wind or the water.
The back of his skull caved in as though he had
fallen back, drunk. Yes, someone could have hit him,
killed him. We all knew how. Who'd do such a thing?

Afterword

These poems owe a substantial debt of gratitude to the custodians of the National Records of Scotland. The Scottish records are invaluable not simply in setting out the basic facts (birth, death and marriage) for individuals, but also proving census, parish courts and other information—as well as a major collection of maps—that make the task of reconstructing the lives of individual Scots not only possible but (comparatively) easy.

As alluded to in the introductory poem, this small collection takes as its starting point the death certificates of a number of my direct ancestors (and one or two other close relatives). Each poem tries to imagine itself into the thoughts of its subject/speaker. The guiding principle (other than chronology) is to develop a mosaic that gives a small sight of Scottish social history, primarily in the late 19th and early 20th centuries.

The language used is (mostly) standard English, while recognising that a number of the speakers would have used Scots or Doric. I leave it up to the reader, where they can, to imagine the speakers' voices as working class Edinburgh or coming from the north-east or west of Scotland.

www.ingramcontent.com/pod-product-compliance
Ingram Content Group Australia Pty Ltd
76 Discovery Rd, Dandenong South VIC 3175, AU
AUHW020721050325
407891AU00005B/33